E.F.T in Your Pocket.

tional

Freedom.

By

Isy Grigg.

EFT in Your Pocket

ISBN 978-0-9549222-2-1

Copyright © 2005, 2007, 2009 by Isy Grigg

3rd Edition Reprinted July 2009

Published and Distributed in the UK by:

New Vision Media Publishing

EMAIL: publishing@newvisionmedia.co.uk

WEBSITE: www.newvisionmedia.co.uk

In writing this book, the author only offers general information to assist in the journey to emotional and physical well being. The author and publisher assume no responsibility for your actions or outcomes.

Having stated the above, the author would like to encourage you to use this book to help yourself and to share it with others. All we ask is that you give fair credit to the author and respect the copyright.

Originally Printed in the UK by T.J. International Ltd

This edition printed by Pepper Communications Ltd

EFT™
A Universal Healing Aid.

Thank You Gary Craig

Gary Craig took a complex and, to the majority of people, expensive Meridian Therapy, pared it down, refined it, named it **Emotional Freedom Technique** and sent it out into the world. He has made **E.F.T.** accessible to everyone. He actively encourages experimentation and applauds innovative new uses of this technique. He is a fantastic teacher who really does cheer at his students' achievements. Since coming into contact with **EFT,** I have effortlessly cleared umpteen, age long, emotional issues and tackled numerous physical symptoms in my life. So I have a lot to thank him for.

For in-depth study of **E.F.T.**, I strongly recommend looking up his web site:

www.emofree.com

This EFT oriented book is provided as a good faith effort to expand the use of EFT in the world. It represents the ideas of the author and does not necessarily represent the complete, standardized EFT training offered at:

<u>www.emofree.com</u>

Important note:

While EFT has produced remarkable clinical results, it must still be considered to be in the experimental stage and thus practitioners and the public must take complete responsibility for their use of it. Further, Gary Craig is not a licensed health professional and offers EFT as an ordained minister and as a personal performance coach. Please consult qualified health practitioners regarding your use of EFT.

Contents.

Why E.F.T.?

Most of us can think of areas of our lives which could be improved, if we were able to make changes to our physical or emotional condition. It may be something in our lives that we no longer want to experience, such as Lack of Confidence, Jealousy, Anger, Grief, Sadness, Guilt, Phobias or Depression etc. Maybe some events from our past keep coming back to haunt us.

Or it may be a physical pain that holds us back, such as joint pain, headaches, stiffness, intestinal discomfort, constipation, insomnia, or back problems to name but a few.

Well, for the time and effort it takes to learn and apply **E.F.T**, it really is worth experimenting!!

<u>Negative Emotions</u>

When a child throws a tantrum and is allowed to kick, shout and become red in the face, it is likely that, by the time they have finished, they will have exhausted all of that emotional energy and so have no need to suppress or store it.

However, as we get older we learn that many forms of behaviour and emotional outpouring are not acceptable. We learn not to express these feelings, and instead we suppress them. We learn to bite our lip, hold our tongues, walk away, say / do nothing, make an excuse, in fact we will do anything not to show or express how we really feel, for fear of disapproval. So where does that leave us? What happens to that emotional energy?

Just because we deny the existence of an emotion, doesn't mean to say that its associated energy has vanished.

Generally each emotion has its own particular energy frequency, and the body will store that frequency in the physical organ or in the body's energy channels (commonly known as **Meridians**) that are best able to accommodate it, with minimal damage to the rest of the body. Much like tuning into the different frequencies of a radio, so the body does the same. Once stored, for safe keeping, this suppressed energy forms a disruption in the energy field, which in turn causes more negative emotions.

'The cause of all negative emotion is a disruption in the body's energy system" Gary Craig. Founder of EFT

For instance

Organ	Type of Emotion
Lungs	Grief, Sadness
Liver	Anger, Resentment
Kidneys	Fear
Gall Bladder	Resentment, Depression
Small Intestine	Rejection, Shock, Abandonment
Thyroid-Adrenal	Confusion, Paranoia
Spleen-Pancreas	Worry, Low Self Esteem
Bladder	Timidity
Heart	Sadness, Shock
Stomach	Disgust, Despair
Large Intestine	Stuck, Rigid Emotions.

Meridians

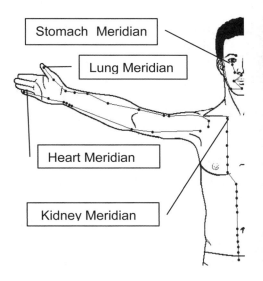

Stomach Meridian

Lung Meridian

Heart Meridian

Kidney Meridian

**This illustrates a few of the
Meridians we use in E.F.T.**

Once we have developed disruptions in the energy system, it is only natural that our emotional / physical responses are altered accordingly. This is when like attracts like, and the body stockpiles these emotional responses. We eventually reach a point where the physical body begins to protest, our emotional state is in tatters or we take a long hard look at ourselves and say:

'Enough! ..... Time to make some changes'

'How?' .... *Let me explain!*

Bear in mind that **disruptions in the body's energy system** will intensify and perpetuate negative emotions.

<u>Time for change!</u>

Now that we understand the principle that a disruption in our energy system can cause us to feel 'less than', we can begin to take counter measures. By removing these limiting disruptions from the body, in a simple and often permanent way, we can begin to reach our full potential.

This is simply a matter of applying a pulse of energy through the energy channels of the body, to neutralise the stored disruption, by gently tapping on 14 Meridian points of the body.

Imagine how liberating it would be if we could just clear these disruptions as soon as we realised their impact on us! Well now it is possible, using the following, very simple technique. So read on ....

Overview

Using EFT involves the following simple steps:

1. **Gauging S.U.D's** –

How strongly do you feel the issue?

2. **Setup Statement** –

Putting your feelings into words

3. **The Basic Recipe** –

Tapping the Meridian Points

Gauging S.U.D's

When a negative emotion (disruption) becomes apparent, the first thing to do is to establish just how strong the feeling is, in order to monitor the progress as **E.F.T.** is applied. This is called gauging the '**Subjective Units of Disturbance**' or **S.U.D's** for short.

To do this simply give the emotional or physical intensity a number, between 0 – 10, with 10 being a very strong feeling and 0 being a very weak or non-existent feeling. (See illustration)

For instance, if your toothache is excruciatingly painful, you may give it a **S.U.D's** level of 10. On the other hand, if it is only a slight dull ache, you may choose to give it a 4.

Subjective Units of Disturbance

(Or **S.U.D's** for short)

10 (Strong/Intense)

9

8   How intensely
            do you feel
7   the feeling, on
          a scale of
6

5   0 – 10?

4   Where are
          you right
3   now? Make a
          note of it
2

1

0 (Little/none)

Likewise, if your stress levels are reaching a crescendo, then a **S.U.D's** level of 9 or 10 may be appropriate, whereas on a normal day you may only feel stressed to a level of 2.

With a little practice, you will find it becomes second nature to gauge your feelings from 0 – 10 as soon as you identify them.

Whenever you use **E.F.T**, there is a tendency to 'forget' just how strongly you experienced things initially, so it is always a good idea to score your **S.U.D's** levels before and after applying **E.F.T.** to help you monitor your own progress.

Set-up Statement

With your **S.U.D's** level established, it is now time to put your feelings into words, and create your statement.

For instance, in the case of stress you may say to yourself, *'I can't handle this any longer'* or *'I can't think straight'* or *'I'm tearing my hair out'*.

Likewise, in the case of physical pain such as a toothache, you may find yourself referring to it as *'I'm suffering this screaming pain'* or *'my jaw is pounding'* or *'this sickening throb'*. You may even be thinking *'This ****** pain is killing me'*. The most important thing is that you use YOUR words to create the perfect statement for you. (even if that includes strong language)

These words / sentences are referred to as '**Reminder Phrases**"

So remember the **Set Up** 'Sandwich'

- 1st slice of bread = **Even though...**

- The filling = Add your **Reminder Phrase** (the words, sounds, or expression to describe the feeling you want to get rid of)

- 2nd slice of bread = **...I deeply Love and accept myself.'**

You may find that saying

'...I deeply Love and accept myself' sticks in your throat. That is okay...say it anyway. If it becomes unbearable you can change the statement slightly and say something like;

...I am <u>willing to learn</u> to deeply Love and accept myself.

Or you could use this as an opportunity to change that response and say;

'Even though..

I hate saying I deeply Love and accept myself,

..I am willing to learn to deeply Love and accept myself'

With a bit of practice it will become easier. The wonderful thing about **E.F.T.** is that it is an incredibly forgiving technique and very difficult to get completely wrong.

You can try it on just about any and every issue that you encounter and know that you have nothing to lose.

Nearly ready!

You have your statement all worked out, which will help you stay focused on the feeling you want to change, so now you are ready to begin tapping the series of Meridian points.

Using the tips of the index finger and the middle finger together, practice tapping in blocks of 5 – 7 taps and let your own rhythm develop. This will help when you begin tapping on the body.

Also bear in mind that firm tapping, (avoid bruising yourself) will generate a better overall effect on the Meridian point, and in turn the issue you are working on.

The Basic Recipe

The basic recipe is made up of the following components:

- **The Setup** –

Counteracting Psychological Reversal.

- **The Sequence** –

Tapping the Meridian Point sequence.

- **9 Gamut** –

Balancing the Creative and Logical sides of the brain.

- **The Sequence** –

Tapping on Meridian points again.

Psychological Reversal (P.R.)

Psychological Reversal is the term used to describe a subconscious level of self sabotage or hidden benefits. This can take the form of negative thinking, denial, social / cultural dogmas, disbelief, or even the desire to keep things as they are.

The simplest example of **P.R.** is in the struggle we all go through to give something up such as chocolate, tobacco, alcohol etc. The conscious part of us says NO to that chocolate biscuit and yet there is another part of us that quietly nags in the background saying all sorts of things that will dissuade our self discipline until we finally give in.

Things such as; *'Go on. One won't hurt'* Or *'I can give chocolate up tomorrow'* are common.

Similarly, in cases where weight loss seems elusive despite genuine efforts, the **P.R.** may be something as simple as being scared of becoming slim, in which case there is a hidden benefit to being overweight. This is not something that is instantly recognised or acknowledged, however this **Psychological Reversal** would be enough to halt someone's weight loss very effectively.

Each round of **E.F.T.** begins by eliminating any potential **P.R.** These points are called the **"Karate Chop'** and the **'Sore Point'** and are discussed more in the next few pages.

The Sequence

From this point onwards you only need to repeat the **Reminder Phrase** of the **Setup Statement** (The filling of your sandwich).

If any of the following points, (with exception of the sore point) are tender, just place your finger tips on the spot. Hold for the time it takes to say your **Reminder Phrase**, followed by a breath, and move on to the next point as normal.

It's worth mentioning that any point that is tender may be holding a disruption. You may find it interesting to read what that Meridian point relates to, on the following pages.

This may also help you with future setup statements.

Eyebrow Point

This point is referred to as **E.B.** (eyebrow) and is located at the point where the eyebrow and bridge of the nose meet. It stimulates the **Bladder Meridian,** which will help to release fear, generate higher levels of courage and increase energy levels.

It is a good point to remember for times when you are unable to carryout the entire round of **E.F.T.** but need help to reduce fear.

From this point on, you only need to repeat the **Reminder Phrase** of your statement, as you tap on the following points. (Softly enough not to bruise yourself, but at the same time, firmly enough to stimulate each meridian point)

Under Nose (U.N.)

Tapping this point will help reduce panic.

Chin

The **Ch.** point is located below the lower lip. Look for the natural crease between chin and lip and that is the perfect place to tap.

Sometimes referred to as the **Conceptual Vessel,** it is effective for helping to overcome shame and releases birth trauma.

This point, tapped simultaneously with the **U.N.** point is great for getting energy to circulate around the body. So a good one if you need a boost.

I'm sure you know the form by now, but just in case. Repeat your **Reminder Phrase** once, as you tap 5 – 7 times.

Chin (Ch.)

This point will help overcome shame and helps release birth trauma.

Collarbone

The **C.B.** point is located along the underside of the Clavicle about 2 cm left or right of where a man would knot a tie. If you are not sure about this one, you can bunch all of your fingertips together and tap a larger area just to be sure.

Stimulating the **Kidney Meridian**, will help to neutralise fear and can assist in increasing willpower and reducing feelings of dread

This is a very useful and discreet point to use at anytime. Especially when you find yourself in a public place and you need a little help.

Tap this point 5 – 7 times as you repeat your **Reminder Phrase**.

Collarbone (C.B.)

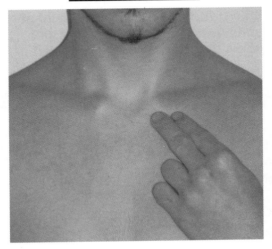

Increases willpower.

This point is incredibly effective and discreet and therefore it can be used at any time on its own.

<u>Under Arm</u>

The **U.A.** point is located under the arm, in line with the nipple and directly below the armpit.

This stimulates the **Spleen Meridian** point and helps to speed up thinking processes, aids concentration and reduces worry. It also has a positive effect on energy levels and decision-making.

As always, repeat your **Reminder Phrase** once, as you tap rhythmically 5 – 7 times.

Under Arm (U.A.)

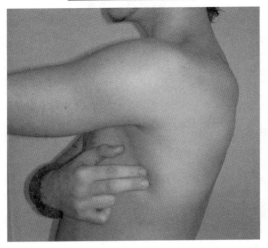

Speeds up the thinking process and sharpens concentration.

<u>Below Nipple</u>

The **B.N.** point is the **Liver Meridian** and is located 2 cm's below the nipple (men) or along the crease of the underside of the breast where the ribs can be felt, in line with the nipple (Women)

Although this point is optional it is a great one for Anger / Frustration issues, so try to use it accordingly.

When this point is stimulated it encourages a more positive outlook and helps in being more receptive to humour and happiness.

Tap the usual 5 – 7 times as you repeat your **Reminder Phrase**.

<u>Below Nipple (B.N.)</u>

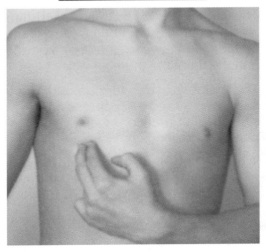

B.N. is a powerful point to help combat anger.

Thumb

The **Th.** point is for the **Lung Meridian** and is located on the outer edge of the thumbnail, between the first knuckle and the tip of the thumb.

This point is useful for cases of grief, sadness and depression. It significantly reduces these types of negative emotions.

When stimulated this point is very effective in allowing a more vital and positive energy to take its place.

This is the first of 5 points on the hand (Other than the **K.C.** point of the **Set-up**) Continue to repeat your **Reminder Phrase** once, whilst tapping (5 – 7 times) on all of the following points on the fingers.

Thumb (Th.)

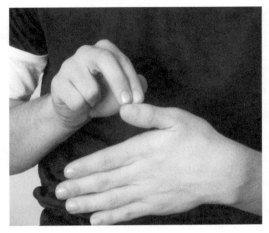

This point is very useful for counteracting feelings of grief and sadness.

Index Finger

The **I.F.** point is linked to the **Large Intestine Meridian**. This can be found at the side of the Index finger closest to the thumb, between the first knuckle and the tip of the finger, next to the edge of the nail.

This point can help to release 'held in' emotions such as guilt and / or melancholy over the past etc. (This point can also help alleviate constipation).

When tapped, this allows a release both literally and physically, to take place, enabling the individual to become more optimistic about the 'now' and the future.

Tap the usual 5 – 7 times along with your **Reminder Phrase**.

Index Finger (I.F.)

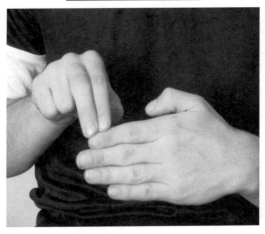

This point allows physical and emotional release to take place.

Middle Finger

The **M.F.** point is linked to the **Circulation-Sex Meridian** and **Heart Governor**. There are two points that could be tapped. The easiest to remember is on the side of the nail closest to the thumb, and the second is on the tip of the finger. However because you are using the tip of the middle finger of your other hand to tap with, you may not feel this to be necessary.

Once stimulated, this point can help with issues of low self esteem, jealousy, sexual problems etc.

When the disruption is cleared it will allow for a more positive outlook based on happiness and humour.

Tap the usual 5 – 7 times along with your **Reminder Phrase**.

Middle Finger (M.F.)

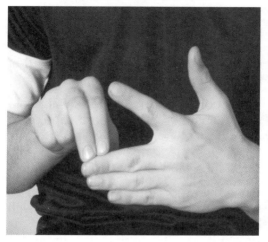

Good for low self esteem.

After tapping this point bypass the ring
finger and go onto the Baby finger.

Baby Finger

The **B.F.** point is associated to the **Heart Meridian.** You will find this point at the side of the nail of the little finger, closest to the thumb, between the first knuckle and the tip of the finger.

This point when tapped will help address issues of the heart. It helps to overcome emotions such as loneliness, anger, heartbreak, arrogance, and shock.

Once cleared, the ability to bring in Unconditional Love along with empathy and compassion is heightened. This point also improves long-term memory.

Tap the usual 5 – 7 times along with your **Reminder Phrase**.

Baby Finger (B.F.)

Heightens compassion and empathy.

This is also a great point for chest pains

Karate Chop

The **K.C.** is the point that you used during your **Set up**. This is linked to the **Small Intestine Meridian** and is located at the fleshy part of the side of the hand.

When a disruption is held in this Meridian it can lead to feelings of self-loathing, lack of confidence, anxiety, as well as difficulty in making choices.

When tapped, not only is it used for **Psychological Reversal**, it can also have very beneficial effects such as improved confidence, clear thinking, and increase self esteem.

This is also useful for overcoming shock.

Tap the usual 5 – 7 times along with your **Reminder Phrase**.

Karate Chop (K.C.)

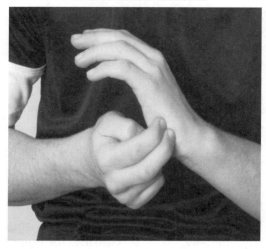

This is another discreet point to tap and will increase levels of confidence.

Gamut Point

This is the point to tap in place of the side of the nail of the ring finger. The **G.P.** is the **Triple Warmer / Thyroid Meridian,** which is located on the back of the hand between the bones of the little finger and the ring finger, just back from the two knuckles. When tapped, this point counter acts loneliness, depression, physical pain, despair and resentment.

It has beneficial effects on the ability to communicate and eases socialising.

Whilst tapping this point gently and rhythmically, the **9 Gamut** formulas should be carried out as described next.

<u>Gamut Point (G.P.)</u>

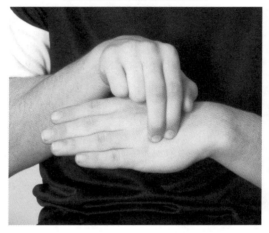

This point counteracts depression and physical pain.

> Tap this point whilst simultaneously carrying out the **9 Gamut** Sequence.

9 Gamut

This series of 6 eye and 3 verbal moves will stimulate both sides of the brain along with motor neuron functions. Keep your head still as you do the following;

1. Eyes shut.
2. Eyes open.
3. Look hard down right.
4. Look hard down left.
5. Eyes in a clockwise circle (as though looking at the numbers of a clock.
6. Eyes in an anticlockwise circle.
7. Hum a few seconds of a tune.
8. Quickly count 1 – 5 (logic left brain)
9. Hum a few more seconds of the tune. (Creative Right Brain)

9 Gamut

CLOSED	Eyes Closed.
OPEN	Eyes Open.
↙	Look hard left.
↘	Look hard right.
↻	Move eyes in a circle.
↺	Now the other way.
	Hum 1 bar of tune.
1 2 3 4 5	Count quickly to 5.
	Hum tune again.

Sequence Part 2

Having completed the **9 Gamut**, it is now time to go on to tap all the points on the face, body and fingers in sequence once more, in order to complete the full **'Round'** of tapping.

(**E.B.**) Eye Brow Point, (**S.E.**) Side of Eye, (**U.E.**) Under Eye, (**U.N.**) Under Nose, (**Ch.**) Chin, (**C.B.**) Collar Bone, (**U.A.**) Under Arm,

(**Th.**) Thumb, (**I.F.**) Index Finger, (**M.F.**) Middle Finger, (**B.F.**) Baby Finger, (**G.P.**) Gamut Point, (**K.C.**) Karate Chop.

Repeating the **Reminder Phrase** (your wording in the **Set Up Statement**) and tap all the points, 5 – 7 times each, again.

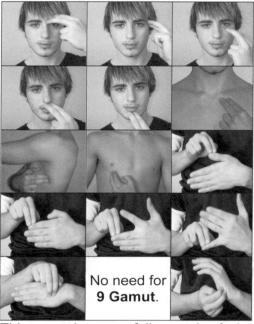

No need for **9 Gamut**.

This completes a full round of the **Basic Recipe**.

Gauge your S.U.D's level again!

- Take a moment to think about the issue you have been working on.

- Try and recreate the same intensity you felt before tapping.

- Do you feel the same?

- Is it a stronger or weaker feeling?

- Give it a number between 0 – 10

- Compare that number to the **S.U.D's** level you felt at the start.

- Keep a record of issues you decide to work on. Make a note of your **S.U.D's** level before and after tapping

You will find that over time the issue you have just worked on will fade from your memory. So much so that you will begin to doubt that there ever was a problem in the first place.

So how do you feel now?

10
9
8
7
6
5
4
3
2
1
0

What do you feel now?

Is it a similar feeling?

Is it a new feeling?

Where are you, right now, on 0 – 10 scale?

Tree Felling or Hedge Trimming?

If you can still feel the emotional or physical feeling, even though the intensity has dropped, then it is a good idea to do a little more in order to clear yourself of this issue completely. A bit like **Tree Felling**, keep tapping until the issue is down to zero.

So, begin tapping again on the **Karate Chop** (side of the hand) and adjust your statement to include *'…this remaining….'*

For instance, you may have originally gauged a headache at 7 and your statement was …

'Even though…

…I have a thumping headache…

…I deeply Love and accept myself'.

If you gauge again and notice that your intensity had dropped, then adapt your statement to be as follows.

'Even though …

…I have _some remaining_ thumping headache…

… I deeply Love and accept myself'

and complete another round.

On the other hand you may have found that the original feeling has paled and another feeling has become more apparent. This can be like **Hedge Trimming** as in taking the tops off a number of issues / feelings to create overall relief.

For instance, your head may no longer be thumping as badly as before and instead you notice that you have a dull ache behind your eyes. This is sometimes referred to as '**chasing the pain**' and can be used on all sorts of symptoms. So gauge the feeling and create a new statement for the new sensations.

'**Even though**…

…*I have a dull ache behind my eyes*…

… **I deeply Love and accept myself.**

Complete a round and gauge again.

Remember that **E.F.T.** is not limited to physical pain. It is astonishingly effective on all manner of emotions, blocks, fears and beliefs. You have nothing to lose, and everything to gain!

TRY IT ON EVERYTHING!

Peeling an onion or an orange?

Most therapies liken emotional issues to an onion, where each layer has to be peeled away before reaching the next. (And can involve a lot of tears)

However, when using **E.F.T**, emotional issues resemble more an orange. Once past the outer skin, an orange is made up of many segments. The same applies to emotions.

For instance, you may start tapping for grief, and then find that as you tap, you begin to notice that there is more to it than a single emotion. You may find a segment of loneliness, another of fear, another of anger and so on. The beauty of it is that you can work at your own pace, on whichever segment you want, without further tears and trauma.

So be aware of the segments or aspects that contribute to the overall feeling that you are working on, gauge the new aspect / segment, adapt your statement and tap for it.

To help you to get the ball rolling, look through the following examples and pick the most appropriate statement for your given issue. As you tap, you will probably become aware of your own specific terminology.

Remember to gauge the physical or emotional intensity from 0 – 10 and be as specific as you can (in your own words) with your **Set Up** statement and **Reminder Phrase**.

Remember that if you still feel some of the original disturbance having completed a round of **E.F.T**, then complete another round of tapping, using a modified statement to work on 'this remaining feeling'.

It is always a good idea to try and reduce a physical or emotional feeling to zero intensity if you can. (**Tree Felling**) However, if you find yourself shifting from aspect to aspect, then just go with it.

Try to revisit the original issue every now and then, if for no other reason than, to test the effectiveness of all your efforts. It is generally a pleasant surprise to realise just how differently you feel.

Examples

The examples on the following pages are to help to get you get started in using **E.F.T.**

You can use these as the basis for creating your own **Set Up Statements** and **Reminder Phrases**.

Being candid and honest when putting your feelings into words will really pay dividends. Try to avoid editing your thoughts / reminder phrases just to make it sound more palatable. Tell it like it is!!!! even if that includes strong language.

And remember… Play and have fun with this, allow yourself to get creative and pay attention to the results.

Fear

Fear of known things is quite straight forward. Break down the ingredients of your fear. Is it specific? Do you only feel fear under certain conditions I.e.

Even though….

…being in the house alone scares me….

…I'm too frightened to drive in heavy traffic….

…I'm scared of heights….

…**I deeply Love and accept myself**.

List your fears. Gauge each fear 0 – 10, and prioritise anything with a **S.U.D's** level of 7 and above.

Known fears are easy issues to test. So why not tap and then test how you feel towards what scares you.

Sometimes fear is caused by the belief that you can't achieve something. Fear of public speaking for instance. It may be that you fear stuttering, or being laughed at, or simply not remembering what you are there to say.

Even though…

…I will be laughed at…

…I'll forget what to say…

…I can't do it…

…I'm scared to try…

…I think I will fail…

…I can't cope with success…

…I deeply Love and accept myself.

Remember also, that some fears are caused by the unknown, or the imagined.

Even though…

…I don't know what scares me…

…I jump out of my skin at any noise…

…I might get hurt…

…I can't cope with this…

…I deeply Love and accept myself.

Maybe your fear starts in the body.

Even though….

…every time my heart pounds I fear the worst…

…What I'm feeling in my body frightens me…

…I can't catch my breath…

…I feel this fear in my body…

…I deeply Love and accept myself & my body.

<u>Depression.</u>

If there is a specific cause for feeling depressed, such as bereavement, redundancy, etc then start with the most obvious statement and see what starts to emerge. e.g.

Even though…

…I've lost my job…

…My partner has left and I'm heartbroken….

…My children have left home and I feel abandoned….

…????? has died…

… I am overwhelmed with responsibility…

…I deeply Love and accept myself.

If not, here are some examples to get you started;

Even though…

…I want to curl up and hide…

…There is no colour in my day / life…

…I can't bring myself to do anything about this depression…

…I can' t / won't face people…

…It is easier to give in to this than to fight…

…What's the point...

…Nobody cares…

…I'm not worth caring about…

…I deeply Love and accept / forgive myself

<u>Constipation.</u>

Sometimes a **Set Up Statement** can be worded in such a way as to address emotional as well as physical states simultaneously.

Even though...

...I can't let go...

...I need to keep everything in....

...I want to hold on to all the old stuff...

...Letting go is scary...

...I can't risk losing control...

...It's painful to let go...

...My body hurts because it's so full...

...I don't recognise the need to let go...

..I deeply Love and accept my body.

Headache

Apply **E.F.T.** to the specific symptoms. Describe your head pain as accurately as you can and use these descriptions in your **Set Up Statement**.

Even though…

…My head is pounding…

…My temples are throbbing…

…It feels like knitting needles in my eyes…

… I deeply Love and accept myself.

Are there any situations in your life right now that are causing you a headache? If yes, then work on these feelings as well as the physical symptoms. e.g.

…My head hurts just thinking about this…

<u>Back Pain</u>

Remember to use <u>your</u> words rather than a medical label. So instead of saying;

'Even though I have this sciatica I deeply Love and accept myself'. You may find it more appropriate to say;

Even though I have this horrible tingling pulling sensation down my leg, I deeply Love and accept myself.

You could also tackle things like;

Even though…

… I feel guilty that I can't help my wife / boss / workmates / with the heavy work...

…I keep forgetting to bend my knees when I pick things up…

… I deeply Love and accept myself.

Shyness / Self Confidence

These types of issues can be rooted in what you believe other people think of you, as well as what you think of yourself.

List how you think others see you.

List all the 'Less than' characteristics you believe you have.

List all the reasons why you believe others are better / superior / more confident, than you.

Gauge your **S.U.D's** level for each item on your lists from 0 – 10 so that you can prioritise them. Make your **Set Up Statement** and begin tapping.

Have a look at the following examples;

Even though…

…I can never think of anything interesting to say…

…I'm scared that I will be laughed at…

…Everyone thinks I'm stupid / silly / clumsy…

…I will stutter if I try to talk…

…My throat closes up / dries up when I try to speak…

…I will blush / go red in the face if anyone looks at me...

…I'm not good enough to mix with these people…

…I feel 'less than'…

…I deeply Love and accept myself.

Physical Pain

Isolate the thoughts you have regarding the physical pain and incorporate those words into your **Set Up Statement**. You may find that when describing the pain to friends or Doctors, you have a favourite expression, so use that in your statement.

Even though….

…I have a sharp pain…

…This feels arthritic and sore…

…I have a burning pain in…

…I can't stand this anymore…

…I will always have this pain…

…There is nothing that I can do about this…

…My doctor said there is nothing that can be done…

…Every time I do (????), it hurts / gets worse…

…This pain feels like needles…

…It's like a stabbing pain…

…I have to live with this…

…All I want to do is cry it hurts so much…

…I deeply Love and accept my self and my body.

Be as specific as you can. Describe the pain and use that description in your statement. Maybe the pain causes you emotional reactions, so work on those too.

Another way to tackle physical pain is to look at common phrases. Do you find yourself saying / thinking things such as I.e.

I can't handle this. = Hand / wrist / forearm.

This is doing my head in. = Headaches / Migraine / Eyesight.

This situation is a pain in the neck = Neck / Back of Skull / Shoulders

So give a little thought to some of your regular internal / external statements.

This concept can also work in reverse.

If you have a physical pain in the neck, take a look at your life and see if there is a situation / person that is a literal pain in the neck. Tap for it and see what happens. Who knows, it may work!

Questions and Answers.

Q. I find it hard to stay in the 'feeling' so when I have to gauge I no longer feel anything. Does this matter?

A. This is very common. Most people have learnt to bury their feelings very quickly and efficiently. Apply **E.F.T.** to the issue anyway; using the thoughts you had during the original feeling. Go over the events / memories the next day and see if you feel any different. Alternatively you could say;

Even though *I have buried (describe what you were feeling) right now* **I deeply Love and accept myself.**

Or

Even though *I feel (describe the feeling) when I think of / do / say / etc* **I deeply Love and accept myself.**

Q. No matter how much I tap, I don't feel any different.

A. First, drink a large glass of water. If you are hydrated, then your energy system will be much easier to work with. Give yourself a moment and try again. If there is still no change then it's time to check your statement. Is it your words? Is this how you *really* refer to this issue? Are you gauging the same issue or has it shifted to another segment / aspect. This can happen without realising. For example

You may be applying **E.F.T.** to the fear of attending a job interview. So you start with..

Even though *I am really nervous about the interview* **I deeply Love and accept myself.**

However the nervousness would have a number of aspects such as; *'What am I going to say'* or *'What if they don't like me'* or *''Will I get there on time'* or even *'What if I can't do the job'*. So work on each aspect as you think of it.

Q. I have checked my statement and I still don't get results.

A. This is very rare. However, occasionally, certain toxins can slow **E.F.T.** down to a crawl. These toxins can be in the form of certain substances such as wheat, sugar, caffeine, certain herbs, tobacco, pepper, perfume, nicotine, dairy products & corn. So avoid these things for a day or two and try tapping again.

By persistently applying **E.F.T.** to your issue, symptoms will eventually fade or disappear completely.

Q. I keep forgetting where to tap and in what order.

A. The sequence is easy if you remember this simple rule. Question Mark, Dot, Comma.

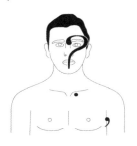

Work your way down the face and body. When you tap the eyebrow, side of eye, under eye, under nose, and chin points, these will form the shape of a question mark with the collarbone being the dot, and under arm is the comma. Then remember to hold your

About the Author

Hi… During my mid 20's I hit rock bottom, Emotionally & Spiritually. All I wanted to do was hide myself in a dark hole and disappear. I moved back home, started reading books, and paying attention to what was going on in my mind. Thankfully it became a turning point for me.

From being an insecure, and to my mind insignificant, human being I have become a happy, fulfilled, optimistic and worthwhile person, and I really like who I am!!!.

Over the years I have had the distinct pleasure of being taught and influenced by the likes of Shirley Wallis, Writer/ Researcher, Margaret Ruby, founder of PossibilitiesDNA, School of Vibrational Healing, and Brandon Bays, author and creator of The Journey and of course Gary Craig's' and his teachings. I thank them all.

To date I have qualified in Energy System Patterning & DNA Activation, Crystal Healing, 'Journey Therapy' and Emotional Freedom Technique. Now, I am a tutor, writer, practitioner, speaker and researcher and I love every minute of it.

I hope you enjoy this book as much as I have enjoyed putting it together.

Happy tapping!!

Isy

Update

EFT in your pocket is now in its 3rd print run and still selling like hot cakes!! I put this down to the way in which it was produced.....on a wave of enthusiasm, laughter, acceptance and love. You are holding in your hands the product of a wondrous collaboration between me and Jamie Wonnacott of New Vision Media. From inspiration in 2004 up until today has been an awesome personal journey for me... one of self discovery, love, acceptance and friendship and so much more. Since EFT in Your Pocket initially went to print in 2005, my life has changed so much; it's hard to know where to begin. I have met with and spoken to hundreds of people, all looking to move forward in their journey to self realisation and I have felt inspired, moved, blessed and privileged to have helped. Thank you all.

Need More Help?

I offer 1 hour telephone sessions which combine intuitive insights and surrogate tapping whilst working in conjunction with your own application of EFT, to make for very powerful breakthroughs.

Call **0800 6118 124** Now

(Free from UK Landlines)

Perfect for reaching deeply entrenched patterns, core issues and belief patterns, that may be holding you back.

> *"My wife found Isy Grigg via Google, and we have both had several EFT telephone sessions with her. She is a superb therapist, and has guided us to new and revealing insights into ourselves and helped to release a lot of old emotional baggage. As well as her supportive and professional manner, she has a great sense of humour. And all from our own armchairs. Highly recommended!"*
>
> Dr. Anthony Levy MB ChB

__Ordering More Copies__

'EFT in Your Pocket' makes an ideal gift for friends and family.

Visit the website for more details:

__www.eft4me.com__

You can also find a wealth of other information about EFT.

__Calling all Practitioners!__

'EFT in Your Pocket' is the perfect tool for practitioners to help clients learn and retain the basic steps of EFT, allowing you to progress further with your client.

We offer a generous discount to practitioners who use EFT.

Visit the website for more details:

__www.eft4me.com__